Gay Romance

Cowboy Romance Novel Featuring A Storyline Where
Friends Transition Into Lovers

*(Stay The Night: A Narrative Of A Straight To Gay
Experience)*

Sebastien Baldwin

Tanner hurried as fast as he could up the stairs after hearing a second scream that was louder than the siren that was still blaring on the porch. He merely hoped that he would be quick enough or that the shooter would be skilled enough to prevent him from being hit long enough to reach the human. As Tanner proceeded up the second flight of stairs, his rear feet hardly made contact with the landing, and the bullet struck him in the hip. It had to be silver because it burnt so badly. With a cry, he fell back into the landing.

Above him a man yelled, "Ha, got you."

The sound of a round being chambered was heard.

Before the man could fire another shot, Tanner hurried to get back around the wall.

Van roared once more, considerably closer this time.

"Shit!" exclaimed the gunman. The weapon then rattled its way down the steps.

Ignoring the agony in his hip and hurrying up the stairs, Tanner let the gun fall to the bottom.

Van and the gunman tumbled in his direction. Tanner was able to jump up and stay clear of them. However, as he struck his damaged hip during his landing, he lost consciousness. Then Parker flew down the steps, buzzing past him.

Despite his strong need to pause and collect his breath, Tanner didn't. He turned and trailed behind Parker toward the pile on the landing that contained blood, golden fur, and black clothing. He briefly recalled the shapes of his fellow pack members when the hunters had removed them. Some of them had resembled what he was dealing with, a mixture of animal and human blood that made it impossible for him to determine whose was where until he was close enough to pull them apart, and it had never worked well. He took a sharp drink and hurried the few steps down to them. Even though he had just recently met Van, he was curious to find out more about the bear because it seemed intriguing. He wanted to try, even if they hadn't had time to establish a genuine connection.

Tanner buried his nose in Van's fur as Parker whizzed past them. It required a moment for him to comprehend that Van was still alive. "Oh Van, my God. Be alive, please. He desired to transform back into a human, but more folks hadn't been checked out of the house. It did not follow that someone was not preparing an ambush, even though no one else had approached them with guns blazing. When he was a wolf, he was far more dangerous than when he was a human.

"Tanner?" Tanner's mind was filled with Van's ideas. It was deeper and different from the relationship he had with his pack, when he had been able to communicate with them mind to mind, even though for a brief while it felt like that.

"Do you have any injuries?" Tanner sniffed about Van and detected only the smell of human blood. However, even that didn't help him unwind.

Van shifted, attempting to separate from the person. "Somewhat bruised, but nothing serious." You made no mention of having telepathy.

"I'm not. I assumed it was you. Tanner found the proposal perplexing, but they were pressed for time. The human authorities would be on their way, siren screaming. If there were any other humans within the house, they had to find them, tend to them, and leave.

Parker was buzzing like a fool, bouncing up and down in front of them.

After untangling himself from the human, Van said, "He's trying to tell us something." "We ought to go with him."

Parker flew halfway down the stairs toward the kitchen and then back up, like a small crazy collie attempting to lure someone to follow. He took off when they began after him. He flew toward the living room rather than the kitchen, but stopped as the icy breeze from the broken window struck him. He changed to a human appearance and appeared skinnier in the nude than Tanner would have predicted. However, he had strong arms and a large chest that seemed to be his sole muscles.

It's so chilly, damn it. Parker gave his arms a rub. "We must have those backpacks." He began moving across the floor in the direction of two backpacks that were lying on the ground next to a large leather couch. "They are carrying guns and laptops." He gave a shrug. However, while traveling here in the Hummer, they were utilizing the laptops. They may contain some helpful information.

Tanner nodded as he stood next to Van, close to the first man he had killed. He remained opposed to become a human. Fire sirens sounded in the distance. They have to move quickly. He took a chance by moving. He had to be able to communicate with Parker and Van. "We must move forward. Van, there's no need to change. I'll take the other backpack if you can take this one. He gave the deceased man next to them a quick glance. Although all the kills appeared to be animal assaults, it might create concerns. Then it dawned on him. The hunters' strategies may be applied to him and his pack. "The two of you move on. I'll destroy this location and return to the van to meet you.

"I am capable of doing that." Van approached and took one of the backpacks and put it to his lips.

"How am I supposed to proceed?" Parker queried. "Going back upstairs to get my clothes is not something I want to do because it's so damn cold outside."

Tanner felt a flash of panic. "You must. If you have a wallet up there with your ID in it, we can't leave them here.

Parker gave a headshake. They robbed me of it. They were putting it in one of the bags when I last saw them.

"So, that functions. Make a shift and enter Van's pack. You can leave here with him. It was the most brilliant thought Tanner could muster.

"All right." Parker's shape drew in on itself, shimmering. It was one of the strangest transitions Tanner had ever seen. There was such a stark disparity in size. Subsequently, he dashed towards the backpack and perched on the zipper, fixating on Tanner.

With only a few glass fragments biting into his feet, Tanner managed to make his way over to them after getting the hint. His hip gave out a painful cry as he grabbed for the pack. He wouldn't worry about the silver bullet now that it was out of his system. With his other hand, he released the zipper long enough for Parker to enter and perch on the laptop's edge before yanking it shut again.

He gave Van a head rub. Tanner hoped he could keep stroking his velvety fur. "Take caution. I'll be back in a short while.

For the first time, the sound of the emergency sirens could be heard over the screamer still on the front porch, making it seem as though they were just a few blocks away.

Van grabbed the rucksack and dashed for the window. Tanner didn't stay to watch him leave the broken glass; instead, he turned and sprinted into the kitchen while swinging the rucksack over his shoulder. The water heater was situated next to the stove in an alcove. They were both gas-powered. He started by kicking the hose that went to the water heater, then he got to the other hose by removing the stove. He ignited both stove burners, causing a spark to ignite and a flame to spread towards the back door. He flung open the door and moved. Tanner leaped the back fence just as the authorities' dazzling lights sliced through the snow. Despite being unbalanced by the bag, he landed on his good leg. The home burst behind him as he staggered to his feet. Heading back to where they'd left the vehicle, he tried his best to dodge the folks that seemed to be suddenly flocking over the area. It wasn't easy with the bullet in him, but he managed. By the time Van arrived to the parking lot, he was about to pass out, despite his desperate thoughts encouraging him to keep going.

His partner. Even though he was still unfamiliar with the man's name, something about it felt appropriate.

"My name is Malachai," he introduced himself, nodding as the attractive man leaned forward on a bar stool. "What do you have in your drink?"

The young man introduced himself as "Johnny Merin," and for the first time, Malachai's name matched his mate's appearance. "I haven't been drinking either," perhaps not in significant amounts. Johnny smiled after giving a shrug. "Neat, make it Crown."

Malachai, laughing, gave the barman the order. Even Johnny was sipping the preferred beverage of Malachai. The indications were becoming a little too obvious to ignore.

"Johnny. Hello. Malachai returned the young man's interest. He decided his name fit him.

With a wordless salute, Johnny held his glass up to Malachai and instinctively threw back the shot. His lips were full of a maddening smile as he turned to face Malachai. Are you prepared to leave?

Malachai laughs softly. He'd been itching to leave for some time. He gave the young man a quick glance before shaking his head. Everything inside of him was yelling at him to lean over the bar and take him right now, so how was he going to make himself look bad to this young man?

Just as Johnny leaped from the bar seat, Malachai trailed closely after. Perhaps a little too close, as Johnny found his ass shoved firmly against Malachai'sgroyne as someone stepped in front of him and he had to take a step back to prevent bumping into them.

With a gentle groan, Malachai put his arm around Johnny, placing his hand on his stomach, and yanked the attractive man closer to him. His cock throbbed in his jeans, pleading with him to shove it inside Johnny now.

The fact that they would be arrested for such things didn't bother his dragon.

The fact that he had finally found his spouse after six hundred years was all that counted. It was getting harder and harder to ignore.

"You are needed," Even Malachai's keen ears could not have heard those three words above the cacophonous noise in there, but he did. He listened to what Johnny said, as he would to whatever his friend said.

That need was literally radiating off the other man, and he could feel it too. Driving him crazy.Far too much encouragement for his dragon.

It's time to blow this off. Now, before everything went even further out of control.

Malachai said, "I'm going to bottom," and although his voice was solid, it didn't seem all that believable. "Please bring me home."

After turning to gaze at him in amazement, Johnny grabbed his hand and pulled him outside, where the silence was considerably greater. But when he got there, he paused and bit Malachai's gorgeous, pouty bottom lip in a way that made her crazy.

The young man looked at him frank and said, "Look, I don't really top." "If that is what you are looking for from me, then maybe this isn't the best idea."

No. No, it wasn't a good plan at all, but Malachai couldn't let his mate leave without a fight. His partner. He discovered that once he had him, he couldn't force himself to let him go. Not at all.

"We'll work things out. Other actions are available to us. Which his dragon thought was an almost comical idea. That night, he was going to claim his mate. He already had one. "You are needed,"

With a gentle sigh, Johnny ran his fingers through his lovely, oily dark hair. It was quite gorgeous, somewhat wavy, and fell to his shoulders.

Malachai wanted to laugh when Johnny said, "When two bottoms get together, it's not always that great." Regardless of what he had done out of need, he was not a bottom. Not really close at all. He had never been.

"Please just bring me home." Malachai raised a hand as Johnny opened his mouth to speak. You won't have any trouble persuading me to take you, but first we should have a conversation. After that, we'll see whether you still desire me.

He was mates with this person. Not a quick fix. He desired to transform into a dragon, encircle the young man with his claws, and take him to a private cave on his own. Of course he wouldn't. He might have once, but things had moved on. That didn't make him any less eager to.

Thus, he would have to caution Johnny about the potential consequences of sleeping with a dragon. He had never revealed his secret to a human before, but his mate was the one who should have known if anyone.

"Are you certain?" When Johnny questioned, Malachai merely nodded.

Yes, he was certain. Never in his life has he been so certain about anything. He only needed Johnny, nothing more.

Malachai ordered, "Take me to your home," and Johnny led him through the briny, ocean-scented night with a lovely smile and a nod.

It took Lucifinil some time to murmur, "I can't eat anymore."

I stood up right away, gave him a quick squeeze on the face, and said, "You have no clue how hard I worked for this? "Complete it, complete it!"

I was asked back to the same private area the following day to serve more dishes.

I was astounded to see, standing at the doorway, not just the two angels from the day before, but also an additional angel with a golden-eyed doll-like face. A group of flaming angels without wings were also present. A man with long, golden hair was seated among these high angels. His face was oddly attractive, his neck gracefully long, and his shoulders broad. Yes, he was the brightest, even if he just sat there and didn't say anything.

"Lu... Lucifer, Your Highness!" I was astounded as I looked at him. "You've actually come to Heshbon?"

I was a little off balance, but only realised that when all the angels' eyes were on me. I bowed my head and continued working. They soon got back to talking, and I gave them soup, one by one. Lucifer rushed out to stop my hand when it was his turn. "I don't need it, thank you."

We hardly touched for a moment, but even so, I could feel a buzzing sensation at the back of my head and in my ears. Maybe I had tightened up a little, since Lucifer raised his head to look at me. His eyes were a captivating deep blue color, so beautiful it nearly seemed unreal.

It took me less than a second to get a little uncomfortable at the next service. I couldn't help but glance in his direction. The unpleasant thing was that he seemed to notice every time I looked at him, his icy disinterest meeting mine.

Eventually, as I was closing things down and getting ready to leave the room, Lucifer said, "Isar, come here."

"Ah, yes!" I quickly walked over to him and bowed. "Is there anything you need, Your Highness?"

"This is for you." I was given six gold coins by him.

"..." I was in disbelief.

"Haven't you ever received a tip?"

"No, no, thank you!" I nodded and gave a forceful shake of my head, saying, "Thank you, Your Highness!"

"Go on, there's nothing more for you here."

In an hour, I earned four silver coins. In one move, he gave me six gold coins. The disparity was too great, a little difficult to comprehend. Six gold coins, nevertheless, could purchase a lot of goods.

I thought about the approaching weekend as I was leaving the room and made plans to go to the market early the next morning to see the freshest ingredients. I wanted to cook a huge dinner at home, invite the mischievous child over, and have a filling feast. The manager stopped me while I was still enjoying my wonderful surprise. With a flick of his wings, he took off and reached out a hand. "Hand it over."

"Huh?"

"The tip you received just now."

I was quite perplexed. "You knew it was a tip, right? It was said to be for me. Why not?

"Tips are not accepted by Black employees. just hourly pay. We gave you this explanation when you first started."

The supervisor bowed with four fingers. "Hand it over."

With wide eyes of disappointment, I watched as he accepted the six gold pieces. I was furious and frustrated when I got home and curled up in bed without saying anything. Lucifinil moved off to take a seat next to me. "What's wrong?"

It is insignificant. I just ran into a few bothersome issues."

After pausing for a while, Lucifinil enquired, "Is it annoying matters or annoying people?"

"Both." My mind jumped to the obnoxious visage of the manager. "I really don't want to see that person again."

After that, Lucifinil remained silent. He just sat at the desk and doodled on his architectural sketches while silently fluttering his tiny wings.

A few days later, I stood by the bank of Lake Siah after school, waiting for the rehearsal to start.

There was a faint rainbow arching over the lake under the brilliant sunshine. Magic-infused treetops formed a canopy akin to clouds, their branches and leaves thin, their flowers bright and dispersed. They looked like the broken stars in the sky.

Wearing a slightly long robe, Lucifinil danced under the sun, chasing after a swarm of butterflies with his short wings fluttering. He looked like a cute golden doll as his little white robe, bathed in sunlight, took on a gentle golden glow that blended with his hair into a single tone.

He never showed more than two wings when he was outside. Considering that he possessed a total of six wings, I couldn't resist posing the question, "Naughty youngster, what are your parents truly like? Even in all the time I've known you, you've never brought up your family."

"... After spending so much time with me, you can't have failed to realize I'm a Seraphim, right?"

Seraphim are meant to have six golden wings, right? Did a child's wings have a different color since his weren't made of pure gold? But all I could do was nod frank to him, "Of course, I've noticed."

"There are two types of seraphim: those who are born as such and those who are elevated later. I was born into the bright morning light of Santa Filia, a Seraphim by birth."

"Ah, our naughty kid is indeed amazing!"

Recalling what I read in the "Scripture," Seraphim were not able to conceive using a womb, unlike feminine angels. Their wings could only beat so fast that they could only produce lesser angels. The level of angel they gave birth to increased with their rank. "So, in the future, you can also create new life by beating your wings?" I said after giving a loud round of applause.

"Right now. Would you like me to make you an Archangel to play with?"

... Are all angels made carelessly higher in rank than me? It appears that there are as many of us humble angels as there are grass blades. I noticed a figure flying in at this precise moment. I covered Lucifinil's mouth in a hurry. "Someone's coming." Lucifinil fought his way free and took off, flapping his wings like a bee.

Metatron was the newcomer, looking even more haughty without his glasses or crucifix. He took a seat next to me, removed his boots, and assumed a more relaxed attitude. "In a few days comes my birthday. Will you be attending?"

The two bears were sleeping off the large amount of fish they had caught and consumed as they lay idly on the lakeshore, their white bellies facing the sun in the most languid way. With all of their enjoyment, the day was passing by far too soon. Miguel's truck would soon be spotted by the evening patrol, which would arrive shortly after sunset. The two men had greatly needed the lovely day that had occurred.

Miguel said, "Come on, baby," and rolled over to stand. It's time to leave. In an attempt to rouse Javier, he pressed his nose into his side, evoking a deep, sour moan from the other bear. Miguel shifted, went to his clothes, and began putting on his jeans.

"I know I know, but neither I nor I think you want to have another run-in with the law."

Javier moved and reached for his, then moaned, "No." "No, I'm not,"

They reluctantly changed and got into Miguel's truck's cab. It was time to return, and he was correct. And Javier wanted to talk to the man on his left about something he was thinking about. He moved into the center of his cab and snuggled onto Miguel's chest after waiting patiently until they passed the border. He declared it his new favorite spot. That exact place that coiled around him, between his arm and chest.

He pressed his face into Miguel and said, "Thank you for an amazing day."

"I'm happy you enjoyed it," he answered. He turned to look down and noticed Javier's hand making small lines on his upper thigh's denim. Even though it was a tiny gesture, he could feel every bit of it, and he was becoming excited.

How come you're down there? Amused, Miguel enquired.

With his fingers digging into his zipper, Javier answered naively, "Exploring." "If that's okay with you?"

Miguel gave Javier a kiss on the top of his head and widened his legs in return. Javier became more daring in his exploration since he knew that was all the approval he needed. Miguel's erection was becoming thicker as he reached for the zipper's head and dragged it down.

Then came his buckle, and as he eventually broke free of Javier's hold, he let out a gasp of delight upon seeing Miguel's turgid manhood. Really, he was a sight to behold. A gorgeous, big cock with a drop of creamy dew exactly positioned at the very tip and a red, mushroom-colored head.

Javier gave in to his desires and bent his head while opening his mouth to lick away the drop of pre-cum that had lured him. He did this by taking only the tip of Miguel's cock into his mouth. Gripping the shaft with his right hand, he allowed his spittle flow down and act as lubricant as he started to give his sweetheart road head. He groaned at the flavor.

Miguel held his breath and kept his eyes on the road as the road head's mounting pleasure threatened to push them into a ditch, even if all he wanted to do was pull over and fuck Javier senseless. Javier had a tiny mouth, but it was wonderfully graceful and talented. He was certain that no one had ever touched certain spots on his shaft as his tongue slipped and dipped into them. Soft and not at all hurried, his hand worked his shaft in a way that made it difficult for him to concentrate on anything but the sensation.

"If you force me to arrive before I'm prepared," Miguel forewarned in a seductive tone. "There will be repercussions."

With a deep, sinister laugh, Javier raised his head for the first time in more than a decade. He teased back, "That's a risk I'm willing to take."

In less than two minutes, he was exploding warmly into Javier's mouth, coating his tongue with his white seed while his hips jerked wildly. His lips had returned to Miguel's sensitive head.

Miguel blew out a "fuck," caressing Javier's hair. It had been such a powerful moment, and Javier had no idea that he'd only just gotten things started.

Javier cast a doubtful glance at the ropes encircling his wrists before glancing down at Miguel's and his nude bodies. Miguel was perched atop him, tightening the last bits of his ropes. There was only focused concentration on his face. Javier was thrilled to learn the end. Javier was even more in love with Miguel because of the heartfelt attention to detail he had shown in making sure the ropes were safe and secure.

Javier questioned, "So what are you going to do to me?"

Miguel was happy with the way the ropes looked and finally let them go, giving a small, sideways smile. What he was going to do to Javier didn't start to make sense until he looked down into his deep brown eyes.

He explained, planting a kiss on his lips, "I'm going to seduce you first." I'm going to torture you after that. I'm going to fuck you until you come, after that.

Javier felt a chill go down his spine as Miguel's seductive voice filled his ears with sensual assurances. Indeed. To every one of those questions, the answer was an unequivocal yes. His mouth moved down Javier's waiting body, still moist and warm. He moved slowly over the thick legs, firm abs, and large pectorals until he reached the core of Javier's ardor. He moved away from his there, planting a single kiss on the tip of his cock.

Javier whimpered, unwilling to let go of Miguel's touch, as he felt Miguel pull away.

Miguel reassured, merely going to the dresser, "Relax." "I just want to take this." He opened the drawer and took out a three-inch-long bright red butt plug and a bottle of lubricant. Obediently lifting his hips and spreading his legs, Javier, who had never really played with toys before, felt that he was up for the challenge of new things.

Miguel gave a menacing chuckle and trailed a playful hand down Javier's left leg. "Very eager! I adore it. To Javier's astonishment, he placed the toy and the lube on the nightstand and turned him over. There was no pinching or tightening of the ropes at his wrist. Rather, they followed the motion and got Javier up on his knees as he supported his front weight against the ropes.

Miguel mumbled, running his fingernails teasingly down Javier's curved back, "Very good." After doing it twice more, he reached up to take hold of Javier's curls and leaned in to whisper in his ear. "Now for the torturous portion."

Javier groaned as he felt the plug slide up into his place of worship, fitting so snugly that he was unable to remove it even if he had wanted to. If it became too strong, he would have to have total faith in Miguel to take it off. But then Miguel pressed the little button on the base, causing strong vibrations to shoot straight through Javier's ass, so any thoughts of that were gone.

Javier groaned and slumped into the ropes, saying, "Oh, fuck." Miguel's hand struck his right cheek hard before he could settle in too much, causing him to gasp. He relieved the pain right away by lightly massaging the area that was stinging. He gave Javier a massage until the pain subsided, then gave him a harder slap, as if he could read his body perfectly.

Javier was shocked at first, but he soon got used to the spankings. He was soon groaning and bringing his behind closer to Miguel in an attempt to get more slaps. In fact, he was getting so excited that he was on the verge of experiencing a strong orgasm. But Miguel stopped and pulled the plug as soon as he begged for more.

He was an attractive Omega. Now that his hood was down, I could make out more of his chiselled features even with the dishevelled hair covering his head and face.

He gazed at my mansion's main hall with wide eyes, and I positioned myself to the side.

With his eyes fixed on his surroundings, he asked me, "This is where you live?"

"This is my place of residence," I chuckled.

"Are you living alone?"

Not at all. Dirk and I share a home.

"Dirk?"

He looked up at me, an eyebrow raised.

"The guy who brought us back here," I laughed. "Never fear. Only a Beta, Dirk. You don't have to worry about him. Right now...

I stepped in his direction and extended my hand.

Maybe you could have me give you a tour of the area.

He swallowed, shifting his throat. I could tell by the expression in his eyes that he was an Omega who was just waiting to be subjugated. Wasting time was not worth it.

"This manner," I uttered.

He trailed me down a lengthy hallway that led to my bedroom and up the stairs. His eyes opened wide with surprise as soon as we entered my large room and he re-examined his surroundings.

"Whoa...,"

His speech faltered. He studied the paintings on my walls, and I got up to turn on a record player nearby. The room filled with the gentle sound of strings.

Nice room, he remarked.

Lucas crossed to the balcony that was attached to my bedroom and peered out at the sea. I took a step towards him and fixed my gaze on his face. He was engrossed.

I pushed open the double doors and said, "Here." "How come you can't see more clearly?"

A gust of cool, briny night air rushed into the space. Lucas shut his eyes and took a long, slow breath. The way he composed himself exuded a sense of peace.

I questioned, "Have you never seen the ocean before?"

He gave a headshake.

"No," he responded. "All I've heard about it are stories."

"Um... You're not like other Omegas. Have you not spent a lot of time in Dirge?

He lowered his head as though he was embarrassed to look at me. He lifted his face back to mine as I rested my hand on his chin.

"Omega, I had a question for you," I said. However... Those are questions, I suppose, that will be addressed later. I would like to ask you another question.

"Yes, master?"

Tell me, Lucas. Have you previously dated a man similar to me?

Once more, he shook his head. A smirk couldn't resist appearing on my lips.

I sighed, "I always like being the first." "Now… If it's okay with you.

The closer I got to him, the less I said. I put my lips to his and closed my eyes. He didn't resist.

He was an indeed an Omega so far.

My tongue swirled into his mouth for a brief second before I pulled my mouth away with a smack.

"You're an Omega," I said. "Show me how you treat an Alpha."

He nodded to me then started undoing my tie. I stood still while he started undressing me.

My tie undone. My jacket removed. My shirt unbuttoned. My belt unbuckled. Lucas frantically started working my clothes off until I was in nothing but my underwear.

I reached down for my cock and stroked myself through the fabric.

"Do you like what you see?" I said, staring into his deep brown eyes.

"Yes, sir," he said with a nod.

"Then why are you stopping."

He fell to his knees in front of me.

He didn't waste another second. He wrapped his fist around me and started pumping my shaft. I sighed a deep breath. My knees buckled slightly but I remained standing.

"Don't stop, Omega…"

I encouraged him to keep going until he finally did what the both of us wanted.

He opened his mouth and sealed his lips around me. The wetness of his tongue lashing at my tip would have been enough to make the weakest Alphas come right then and there.

I reached down and tangled a hand in his messy hair to brace myself.

"I suppose I can do some work," I sighed.

I held his head in place and proceeded to rock my hips back and forth. I moved slow at first, not giving him my full-length. With some Omegas, you never could tell if their throats could handle it.

Every thrust was deeper than the next. The amount of spit coating my shaft made it easier to slide deep inside of him. His gagging sounded desperate, growing louder with every stroke.

"Let's see if you can handle this…"

I reached down with both hands and tightened his hair in my grip. I squeezed his head tight as I plunged the full-length of my swollen cock down his throat. I heard a choked gasp. It filled me with even more pleasure.

I looked down at Lucas. His eyes were shut tight with tears streaking out of the corners. Even though it appeared like he couldn't breathe, he was enjoying it. He wasn't resisting. He just remained on his knees with his arms at his sides while I fucked his throat.

His face was set. The truck carried on eating up the miles. We sat in silence for a long time. Finally he sighed.

"Thanks for telling me, Ryan. I don't blame you for finding me, I'd probably have done the same." His smile was twisted. "So, we need to get acquainted, as we're going to have a few days together while I sort things out."

"I know you don't want me." I had to get it out quickly, or I'd never be brave enough to again. "You could just let me out in the forest or somewhere." I looked out at the mountain. "I can learn to hunt, maybe I can just live as a wolf. They won't find me here." I set my jaw. "Then you can go back and not have to ..."

"So you think that I shouldn't see Chief Fox brought to justice? Do you think I can just forget what you've said?" Brad sounded so angry, so bitter, that I flinched.

Then he glanced sideways at me.

Not at all. The easiest way isn't always the right way, Ryan." He stifled a sigh. "Now I know, I have to do what's right." He stared ahead and the silence drew out.

Then he turned and smiled at me. "So, we're stuck with each other, I'm afraid." His gaze assessed me. "How does that make you feel?"

I thought for a moment. I didn't want to assume that we would become mates, I didn't know whether he wanted to acknowledge we were fated. I was just glad that I could stay with him, at least for now.

"I'm happy for me, because it means you're going to help me. But I'm sorry if I'm causing you trouble." I prepared the little speech in my head before I said it, but my head was swimming and I wasn't sure how he would take it.

"Hmm." His gaze was calculating. "Maybe you need some breakfast." He sounded as if he was musing to himself, so I sat quietly.

A few miles later he turned the truck into a gas station. "Wait here, Ryan," he said as he jumped down from the cab and began filling the truck. Then he swung away from me and walked off to the small shack to pay. I watched as his broad shoulders moved freely and my gaze dropped to his ass and the muscles flickered as he moved, lithe and fast. My cock twitched and stiffened in my pants. God! I was actually spending time with him. Alone with him. I imagined myself on my knees with him behind me, his cock at my hole and I moaned, trying to pull myself from my dream. I bunched the blanket up on my lap to hide my arousal as I saw him walking back towards me, his arms full of packets.

I tried to slow down my breathing as he opened my door and poured the packets into my lap.

"Hold onto these until I find somewhere to stop." He gave me a sharp glance and I worried that he could see the arousal in my face. I felt a bit dizzy and rather clammy. Oh, God! I needed to control myself.

The sound of his door slamming and his car driving away gave me a start. After a few more miles, he turned into a bumpy track, which we bounced around for some time. Then he parked in a little meadow and killed the engine.

There was only the sound of the truck's cooling metal as a deep silence descended upon us.

With a groan, Brad turned to face me. "Go ahead, please. You must consume some food. In fact, so do we both."

Leaping to the passenger side, he turned around. He opened the door and took the blanket off my lap, letting the packages fall all over me. I quickly snatched at them.

It's alright. Every one of them is sealed. He placed the blanket at the base of a massive pine tree, strolled across the clearing. Then he returned. As I descended, he collected the packets. He gave the blanket a nod.

"Please take a seat; I'll just get some water."

His truck had everything he needed, which impressed me. I assumed he was prepared for a lengthy call-out at all times. I saw him move toward me and reach inside the trunk, that hot figure that had occupied my thoughts for so long. I pondered how to win his approval as his mate, but I was persuaded that there was nothing I could do. He would make the choice. All I wanted was for him to have me in his life. I required him. I made an effort to remain composed.

Jonathan knew right once where the scent of wolf hair and ocean breeze was coming from. Jonathan recognized Joel, their server, from the aroma as he approached their table. The most attractive man Jonathan had ever laid eyes on captured his attention. The young man, five and a half feet tall with carefully combed silky brown hair, smelled like an omega, and he knew it. He had the most captivating dark chocolate brown eyes, and Jonathan believed he could not weigh more than one hundred twenty-five pounds. Joel was being introduced by Chase to everyone seated at the table, explaining that they had graduated from the same university located on the Newark, Delaware, eastern shore campus. Jonathan had already gotten up and knocked over his chair, banging hitting Tim's head as he walked around the table to shake Joel's hand before Chase could introduce him. Joel's trembling fingers sank into Jonathan's trembling hand, and a spark of heat shot between the two men. Jonathan nearly toppled over his overturned chair that was lying behind him as Joel's face instantly flushed deep red. He was positive that his anxiety made his wolf erupt from his body and yell, "Hello!" Trying not to look embarrassed, Jonathan instantly turned his piercing brown eyes down towards the table. Chase informed everyone that Joel and he had recently graduated from college together as members of the same nursing cohort. Jonathan questioned Joel's employment at the cafe given that he had recently graduated from nursing school.

Tim leaned to thank Jonathan for the elbow in his eye after Joel had taken their meal orders. When Tim realized what had transpired, he replied, "I take it that you've found your destined partner?" Jonathan answered, grinning broadly, "I hope Chase can tell me more about Joel's life." Are you aware if he belongs to your pack—that is, our pack? I'm positive I felt he was an omega.

"Jonathan, I have been here longer than you. On my first day here, why wasn't I able to find my destined partner? It was Tim. Tim answered, "I'm not sure if he's a member of our pack." However, I had previously seen him at the main pack house. He must consider Chase to be a close friend. Tim said, "You can ask him after dinner, or I will." Alec called out to Jonathan from across the table. We recently learned that you purchased the historic Victorian home located on Timberland Lane in the pack's northern hills. Best wishes. The house is gorgeous, but it's too big. With all that room, what could you possible accomplish?

Jonathan clarified, "I don't intend to be unmarried for the rest of my life. I'm praying to the gods to guide me to my intended partner. When we're ready, we can start bringing a large number of puppies into the house. Jonathan had dreams of owning a large house and meeting his destiny mate, an omega, since he was a young pup. All the puppies he and his partner could handle would make up their enormous family. Jonathan only had one sibling, with whom he never really got along, and his parents were both alphas. "And I intend to welcome other pack members and their families into my home if I don't find my destined partner. Time will tell. In addition, the house requires extensive maintenance, which will take up a lot of my time," he stated. Joel and Jonathan had a brief encounter, but Jonathan knew right away that he was meant to be. He had to have a more private meeting with Joel to validate his suspicion. As Jonathan was serving food to the people sat at the tables by the windows, he could not help but notice Joel.

Since Joel would exchange subtle looks when able, he was positive that Joel saw his demanding gaze and wandering eyes. The employees of the restaurant hurriedly sped up their speed as the bistro patrons gathered at the entrance. Because of the commotion, Jonathan couldn't find Joel. A few moments later, Joel came out of the kitchen, headed toward their table with a big tray slung over his right shoulder. Since helping an omega was in Jonathan's character, he started to stand. Furthermore, Joel wasn't particularly big, so Jonathan assumed it would be difficult for him to carry the tray. However, he quickly realized that he might very probably offend Joel or at the very least embarrass him. Joel turned quickly when he arrived at the table and placed the tray on an open tray stand. Jonathan was practically correct; he would have felt ashamed of himself.

Jonathan excused himself after supper, thinking he would use the bathroom, but he really hoped he would timing it to meet Joel. There was no way he could leave this restaurant without saying hello to everyone. Jonathan realized that Joel must have been taking orders for coffee and dessert as he made his way back to his table. He deliberately reduced his speed in order to catch up with Joel, and he was successful. Joel and he were walking in the same direction. Jonathan walked over to Joel and put his hand on his shoulder, telling him what a great evening it had been. "All right, thank you, sir. I will let the chef know what you said. I'm sure he'll be happy, Joel said with a pleasant smile. "I also wanted to say hello and introduce myself. Are you aware of who I am? Jonathan grinned, wanting to embrace

Joel, give him a kiss on his soft lips, and taste him.

Joel said, "Yes, sir." "You are my fated mate and my alpha; your name is Jonathan."

Tag Group The Lifeguard

Written by Jackie Thrust

I do not consider myself a hero. Though I wouldn't consider myself thus, others probably would. No. I'm a lot of things, but I'm not sure if calling myself a hero is the right term. The thing about me is that all I've ever needed or wanted to do is help other people. My innate wisdom and cool head on my shoulders play a part in it. My broad shoulders and inherent power play a part in it.

It helped that I've always enjoyed swimming. To say that I enjoyed it would be an extreme understatement. I adore swimming. To me, there was nothing more enjoyable than jumping into the water and running lap after lap. It was only fitting that I worked as a pool guard in high school to earn a little extra cash. Naturally, I continued my summer employment by doing the same thing when I was accepted on a swimming scholarship to a university (I won't say which one), only this time it was on the real beach. That was a huge plus because I was able to work on my amazing tan in addition to being in shape.

At twenty-one, I believed that my future held a lot of promise. Even though I wasn't the world's greatest swimmer, I was still very talented and an essential member of my team, and I was getting good grades and making good use of my scholarship at the university.

The problem was, though, that I enjoyed spending those extended summer days at the beach. I enjoyed the attention that the attractive coeds in bikinis gave me.

I also enjoyed surreptitiously glancing at all the attractive, extremely fit guys.

It happened early in the summer, on a Thursday afternoon. The screams came while I was doing one of my routine patrols in the late morning. As my head whirled to the right, I caught sight of him, rather distant. Too distant. It seemed like a rip tide engulfed him, as his head briefly submerged once again before rising to the surface once more. It was not him who was shouting, but a couple of the girls. He was probably too terrified and too far gone to do anything but try to stay afloat.

which, happily for him, he was not succeeding at.

I rushed straight for the water, oblivious to the sand smashing beneath my feet. I felt as though all other sounds had been silenced and my attention was solely focused on the man I needed to save. I was okay with the fact that nothing else mattered. I had a goal, and all I could think of at the time was, "I got you."

You'll be alright, I promise. You are with me. I'll be there. Remain calm.

I swam quickly and forcefully in his direction, cutting to the side of the rip tide to avoid getting swept away. Yes, it wanted too, but as long as I maintained my acute angle, I could outmaneuver the ocean because I knew this beach well.

By the time I reached him, my heart was pounding in my ears, but I didn't care. My priority was ensuring his safety while being dragged back to shore.

A wave hit my head and his head bobbed under the water once more. In contrast to the man I was rescuing, I followed the river and allowed it to push me back before emerging on the other side.

Upon spotting him, I swam the last few meters towards him, my right arm extending to seize him firmly and encircling his exposed chest.

He fought for a little moment before letting go and realizing I had him. I was happy that I wouldn't have to bring him back to shore after letting him pass out.

Although the swim back was hard, my adrenaline kept me going. We swam back towards the mainland at an angle, and he didn't fight me, indicating that he knew exactly what I wanted from him.

We were both back safely on shore only a few minutes after the whole episode began. While my chest was still heaving from the intense exertion, his companions ran up to us.

I eventually got a decent look at him when he coughed a couple times. When his body was submerged in the water and he was drowning, it had been a bit difficult to truly understand him. His eyes were a rich blue, his black hair tasseled. While his friends were swarming around him, he had sand on his brow. As soon as he gathered his breath, he met my gaze and didn't take it.

I felt as though he was Medusa, immobilizing me. My body was heating up instead of becoming immobile, and my heart was beating faster than it had only a few moments earlier, when I had been preoccupied with battling the ocean to rescue this enigmatic hunk's life.

"I'm grateful," he muttered.

I gave a head nod, but I remained silent. My cheeks had reddened. It was not the death in the salt water that I had just rescued him from; it was because of him.

"No issue. I remarked, "Try to be more cautious out there—that undercurrent is a bitch."

I wanted to say more, but decided it would be best to be quiet. So, in order to log the rescue, I turned and jogged back to my station.

As I lay there on my bed, my thoughts kept returning to Nikon. I always found myself staring at the ceiling and thinking about it after spending so much time by myself and wondering what would happen next in my life. I thought back to all the failed relationships I had before, including the times I believed I had found my true love, only to discover that it was all for nothing.

Was I getting a bit depressed? I felt hopeful at times, especially now that I was looking through the various profiles I discovered on this dating app, but occasionally I didn't. After considerable browsing, I came across a website called ClickDesire where I may potentially find someone with whom I could have a one-night stand. I didn't want to raise my expectations, though.

They all shown interest in me by leaving likes on every picture I posted, messaging me repeatedly, and occasionally inquiring as to whether I was speaking with someone else. There was no doubting that I was wanted, but even so, it was really hard for me to go on a date at this time because my thoughts were still on someone else. Of course, that someone else was none other than Nikon.

What on earth was he doing? With my hand reaching under my trousers to grab my cock, I asked myself. With a few strokes, I could picture him falling on me, his lips encircling my magnificent, swishing his tongue around it as he concentrated on its underside. I would get so much pleasure from it that I would probably arrive in record time, I thought, grinning and berating myself for thinking such a thing about someone so innocent, someone so unlike me, someone who was the epitome of a twink.

I inhaled deeply and continued to swipe my finger around the screen, caringssing my gland tenderly, until I happened upon something I had given up on finding.

It was Nokon, and he looked so adorable on his ClickDesire profile. He looked happy in his profile picture, which made me want to pinch his cheeks and be in the picture. I wish I could have, though.

I decided to reload the screen, figuring this indicated he was looking for a mate, only to discover that his profile was vanished.

How in the hell? I questioned myself, swiping the screen once more, wondering what the devil had happened. I quickly discovered that his profile was vanished completely. I realized that I must have dreamt it after blinking twice in a row.

I poked my own shoulder, though, and realized that I wasn't drunk and I wasn't dreaming either.

"What's happening here?" Gripping Mr. Mitch in my palm and staring into his phony, plastic eyes, I pondered myself if he would ever do the one thing I hoped he would one day: respond to my queries when I spoke with him.

It was never going to happen because he was a plush doll. He was little more than a memory from my early years. I remember how hard it was for me to let go of my childhood, so I dragged Mr. Mitch along.

Nevertheless, I returned the plush toy to the bed and continued to swipe my finger around the screen, hoping that Nokon's profile would reappear.

It was completely absent, just like the previous time, and I couldn't help but wonder why.

I jumped from the bed and dropped my phone on the bed before using the restroom. Though I still felt like this was possibly the start of something I would regret, I had to urinate after thinking about Nokon so much and seeing his profile on ClickDesire. I thought to myself, my fingers slowly going up and down my prick, that it aroused me on again, but the age gap was too great.

Is hooking up really that horrible of an idea? With my balls slamming against my hand and my shaft getting thicker and harder, I questioned myself. I started to sigh and spit into the toilet, releasing a stream of my sperm into the water.

I flushed the water and closed the toilet lid, still huffing but a little less than before. I then proceeded to the sink to wash my hands. I made the decision to end whatever was going on after I noticed myself in the mirror.

The motorcycle club's president and vice president were correct. Whatever was going on between Nokon and me would end when I found my fated mate one day.

Saniyah felt as though something had burst inside her mind when he took her hand. She experienced immediate vertigo, lightheadedness, and intense arousal. Saniyah noticed that Drakka was experiencing the same powerful emotion that was running through her body as she stared into his face. His breathing had grown raspy and shallow, and his eyes had enlarged. He was staring at her with a confused yet intense expression.

Beneath everything, she could perceive the unadulterated, primordial want permeating every part of his physique - precisely as it permeated every part of hers.

Before Saniyah knew it, she and Drakka were involved in a passionate, almost frenzied kiss. She wasn't sure who started it. His hands moved over her body, caressing her ass and running down her back. She instantly felt a fire between her thighs that she had never experienced before spark as she felt his thick cock pressing against her tummy.

With her breath as shallow and strained as his, she broke off the kiss and stepped back. Saniyah was horrified the moment she met his gaze and recognized his need and want for her. Saniyah kept herself back even though she yearned to be in his arms and feel him enticing her—or at least, certain portions of her did. Her body trembled, butterflies in her stomach battering her insides as she stared into his eyes and saw the questions rising to the surface.

"What's that?" Drakka enquired quietly. "How are you doing?"

Right now, she was feeling anything but okay. She felt conflicted. ambivalent. She was engaged in an internal conflict and was unsure about which side to support or which side to prevail. She was supposed to be pure till marriage because she was an Angeliym. It was customary for her people. And even though she usually rebelled and rejected the majority of the customs, this was unique in some way. Giving herself over to this man wasn't as simple as Saniyah had thought.

Have I caused you any harm? With concern darkening his features, Drakka questioned.

Saniyah gave a headshake. "Nah," she muttered. "I'm not hurt by you. I'm doing fine.

She had never dated a man, how could she tell him? Telling him that the kiss they'd just had was the first kiss of her life would be impossible. Because of his exceptional beauty and status as a prince, Saniyah was positive that he had slept with more women than he could recall. She was afraid he would make fun of her inexperience or laugh. that her still being a virgin would in any way turn him off.

More than anything, she was afraid he would reject her for it.

She had a deep desire for him. She desired to have sex with this man for physical pleasure. She didn't know what she was doing, though. She has no past to fall back on.

Drakka said, "It's okay if you want to stop." "I promise never to coerce you into doing anything against your will."

She noticed the honesty in his eyes as she met them. She wanted him even more when she realized he meant what he was saying. Even though he was a Dragon Overlord, Drakka was a decent man. He wasn't at all what she had been made to think about the Dragonborn.

However, she believed that she would lose him if she did nothing at all. Frustrated tears welled up in Saniyah's eyes, and she closed her mouth again before opening it to speak. Drakka moved forward, dabbing away her tears with his thumb. He gave her a kind grin as she gazed up at him.

"It's alright," he stated. "We're lacking —"

But I'd like to," she remarked. "That's all there is to it,"

Saniyah bowed her head, wishing she could let out a frustrated cry. But Drakka slowly raised her head so that she was staring into his eyes again, placing his fingers just below her chin.

"What's it?" he inquired.

She let out a sigh. "I have never dated a man before."

It hurt to admit it, and she prepared for him to turn away. to chuckle. to turn her down. But she was completely caught off guard by what he did next. Leaning in, he gently kissed her on the lips. She thought it was fireworks going off in her head, and when she opened her eyes, she saw a gentle blue radiance surrounding them.

Drakka stepped back after a minute and grinned down at her. "It's alright," he stated. With me, you have nothing to be afraid of. Nothing at all.

Saniyah leaned in and planted a passionate kiss on Drakka, as though she was being pulled in by a magnetic force she could not resist. He slipped his hands back up her body, grasping her breasts while their tongues danced and swirled in her mouth. He pinched her taut nipples through the gauzy material of her dress, and she let out a faint groan.

Gently, he took her hand and lowered it to his trousers. She was perceptive enough to see through his pants to what he wanted, and she proceeded to stroke and squeeze his stiff cock. Saniyah tightened her hold on Drakka's cock, causing him to scream and throw his head back. She released him as soon as she saw his response.

She mumbled, "I'm sorry," very fast. "I didn't mean to cause harm."

His smile was uneven. He said, "You didn't hurt me." It was an incredible feeling. Please don't give up.

With a smirk, Saniyah reached down and grabbed his cock by slipped her hand into his pants. She stroked it while holding it tightly. Grumbling, Drakka drew her closer to him and planted a hard kiss on her lips. With his hands slid down to her waist, he lifted her dress. His hands found her bare thighs, causing Saniyah's breath to catch in her throat.

He slid the tip of his tongue down her neck, making her skin feel like it was on fire. With a faint groan, Saniyah tightened his grasp on his cock, causing him to gasp. Even though Drakka's skin felt heated to the touch and appeared to be burning from within, it was nevertheless nice to feel his body against hers. Perhaps it was because he was Dragonborn, with the ability to breathe fire when he transformed into a dragon.

Section 7

I barged through my castle's doors.

The guy Erlendr, standing so close behind me, nevertheless heightened my senses. "Skallagrim!" the overseer of my staff greeted me at the door. "Prepare food and a bed-thrall for my rooms," I replied. "And Yngvild, order all to rest and reconvene at the third hour after noon." We'll organize our defense.

"The villages to the south are safe with us!" Yngvild yelled to the occupants of the castle.

"Hail!" Glory to our King!" said the guards and attendants.

I gave them a wave before heading to my quarters. I noticed that the hostage was staring at me as I turned the corner. His very deep blue eyes resembled those of a newborn human child. Our eyes met. I had to force myself not to leap across the floor, grab hold of him, and pull him into my bed.

But it was not going to work for my new alliance or the new lord I was defending. Even though they could be put down with fire, rebellions were not desirable. Every ally, no matter how human, was necessary if I was to stop Högerdonn.

My skin was still tingling. I was dismayed to see a small, red-haired thrall in my bed who didn't resemble Erlendr as I pushed open the door leading to my room.

8: Approach him.

The voice was crystal clear in my head, like a horn in the early morning. My directives were unambiguous, and it was evident to whom they applied. I walked in the Dragon King's footsteps. I had to talk to him. His justification was insufficient to justify advancing upon my people. He is not my ruler despite this castle, these wealth, and innumerable slaves. I felt a stab of recollection for my servants. When things were more resolved, I would inform my brother that they would be released. They had armed themselves willingly, eager to die for their village even though there was no combat.

My shoulder armor was seized by an arm. I turned aside. It was Yngvild, the woman at the Dragon's right hand.

"Destroyer, release me."

She growled a little, almost like she was laughing, "You keep calling me sorceress, as though you have no sorcery about you."

"I want to talk to the Dragon King."

She stared at me, then at the hallway. She gave a shrug. "You are free to travel wherever you choose; you are not a prisoner here. Remember that. Once you've spoken to your satisfaction, proceed, and Skallagrim will locate your lodging.

She pivoted and strolled along the hallway. The way the thralls scurried out of her way and made the sign against hexing proved that I was right, or at least had to be. She was definitely a sorceress. The soldiers bowed before her as she proceeded, and when a servant brought her a horn of mead, she simply paused to take a sip before instructing the attendant to bring her another. My lips quirked. Maybe back then, we weren't all that different. I would know whether or not we could be allies if I survived to witness her fight.

I strolled down the hallway, taking in the beauty of the masonry. Even though we were indoors, there were cut-out windows in the hallway. I peered through and saw a grand hall below. It was crammed with multiple hearths with smoldering fires and large wooden tables. From someplace below, came the aroma of baking bread. A servant walked by with a flaming candle, and my eyes grew wide. I have always loved the smell of beeswax, no matter how expensive. The raised dais was in the center. It was full of earth, and in the middle of the castle sprouted an ashen tree with spring-green leaves. I raised my head. At the top was a round aperture. Softly, snow fell through it and gathered on the leaves of the trees. It was unlike anything I had ever seen in my life; it was so beautifully simple.

My steps picked up speed. I had no idea what was drawing me onward. I became hurried. There was something I was running against. I turned the corner. There, the double doors with the iron inlay dragon at the end of the hall. That's definitely where he was.

The sound of the double doors reverberating through my palm and down the corridor reached me as I ran over to bang on it. I sensed that someone was looking at me. They had pivoted to observe my mission. Nobody took a response. I rapped on the door once more. It reflected off the walls of stone. My nose was drawn to the scent of incense and musk.

The door gave way slightly. On the other side, the Dragon King stood without a shirt. My cheeks became crimson and heated.

"I'll come back later," I said as I turned to leave.

He answered, "Come in, or did you not knock?" He was teasing me by raising an eyebrow.

He opened the door further. That's when the incense hit me. It was intense and unfamiliar, and it cast a cloud over the surroundings. Glancing passed the Dragon King to his bed, I entered. A thrall with red hair, trimmed to the base of his head, was lying there in his undies.

I turned my gaze from the thrall to the King's windows and said, "I can go."

"Thrall. Go from us.

With a pouting expression, the redhead gathered up his clothes and left the room. Sinking onto a leather chair, the Dragon King took up a drinking horn.

"Mead?"

Indeed, your Majesty. Oh, let me to assist you.

Hurrying to get the cup, I filled his before filling mine.

He said, "Sit."

I did, taking in the mead's lovely honey scent. Was he a frequent drinker? It was an expensive brew. My gaze shifted to his chest. It was a muscular wall. His hips protruded with lines pointing down, barely above his leggings.

I tried to forget about his erection as I returned my attention to the windows. The size of the dragon should not have astonished me, but there he was. I had flirted with a few rural women, but I had never really warmed up to any of them. I was too afraid to try the other option.

This King had welcomed a man into my bed with a thrall that I had never welcomed before. I swallowed. He observed me. The spot on my skin where his eyes touched me felt warm. I faced the wall once more. Cups of all shapes and sizes adorned shelf after shelf. A group? However, what a strange...

He took a sip and asked, "Why are you here?"

I followed suit. It was scented with herbs and delicious. My mouth felt clear and refreshed.

"My brother may have been persuaded by your comments, but I still need to know what's going on. Why gather your forces and attack us? Why right now?

"Your brother was persuaded by my strength, not just my words," he said, scrutinizing me with narrowed eyes. His hand trembled on the table, and I wondered, "And why? For if the Dragon Högerdonn is not driven back, he will slay us all.

I gazed at his quivering hand, marveling at its magnificence and the prominent veins. "Can you please turn him back? You are The Dragon King."

"Yes, I believe we can if we secure our borders. He can decide to go in a different path, leaving those regions to be destroyed.

"You want him to kill other people?"

"As long as my people aren't involved."

I got to my feet, clenching my fist, I said, "This doesn't feel right." His lip quirked and I said, "Your Majesty, if your enemy is what you say he is, then he is a threat until he is dead," maintaining a calmer tone of voice.

He got up, set down his horn on the table, and walked right up to me. He was about five inches taller than me. He approached. Musk and smoke wafted from his body. I retreated a step. He moved forward, drawing nearer to me, and seized my arm. My flesh felt like it was being burned by the fingers that wrapped around it.

"Give it up!"

He snarled, "And you are giving me orders?"

His sharp teeth flashed. He grabbed me with both hands, raised me, and smashed me against the door in a single motion.

"King."

"Your Majesty, when you address me," he murmured, panting heavily. I gazed up into his eyes and he gave me a ravenous look before continuing, "I am your leader, now."

"Yes," I said, leaning my chin up, my feet hovering a few inches over the ground, my shoulder throbbing, and my spine crushed against the wood. I'm not sure why, or why I felt I should. My body was reacting to his roughness, though.

I lifted my face to meet his, and gently touched my lips to his.

The dark lashes of the Dragon King fluttered. He moved back in response, grazing my lips with his full mouth. He was practically tasting to me. My heart was thumping in my ears because we were so quiet. The man then let out a growl that carried up into his chest, accompanied by a low rumbling. His body pressed me up against the door, his hips and chest slamming into mine as his hands gripped my stomach, my legs, and my bottom. He kissed me, and I closed my eyes, eager to forget everything I had ever known, confused and enraged.

I recall loving every minute of fighting goats and chickens as if it were some kind of dream. Their carcasses were palpable in my mouth, and I could taste how easily their flesh broke apart when my teeth tore into it. Even though that was the first time I had remembered anything at all, it still seemed hazy and like it was happening to someone else. I awoke to discover that I was not alone after flashing on the young man that I had an oral examination of the body.

When I awakened in a barn, someone else was resting next to me. His face was turned away from me, and he was naked. The crusted blood on his skin prevented me from identifying the body. He yawned and turned to face me. I was shocked to see that it was the young man I had made the moment enjoyable for.

I'm not sure what happened, Lynn, but the last thing I recall doing was savoring your deliciously sweet hole. Then I wake up here with blood all over me, and you're staring at me like you can't believe I'm still alive." I had no idea what to say. My only option was to seize him and physically drag him out of the barn and down to the nearby lake. This spot had existed here in the 1800s and was now desolate.

We found ourselves splashing in the water, removing the lingering effects of the previous night's events. I started sucking his cock as I searched for any wounds on his body. After spending the night hunting and murdering for survival and pure fun, it was just what I was searching for.

I stopped him when he got too close to the water with two fingers and pulled him to the edge of the river. He gave me a look as if he was having trouble believing that this was really happening as I spread my legs. His cock itched to feel the inside of me, and all memories of why we were in that barn disappeared.

"I have never dated an older woman." Everything happened for the first time, and I wasn't in the right mindset to refuse him anything. He touched me with the tip of his cock, and my body felt like a live wire. My whole body began to quiver. "I don't even care why we were found in that barn together; I just want to fuck you for whatever reason." As soon as the ecstasy subsided, I discovered a bloody peck on his neck. His change was going to take him completely by surprise.

He buried himself in my tight sheath, slipping carefully into my folds so that I could feel every inch. I could feel him filling me like no man had ever filled a woman before, and my body curved around him as if he were intended to be.

"I understand what you're saying, and I believe you should just accept it." He didn't dispute the argument; instead, he kept moving forward and then backward until my head was all that was left inside of me. "Give it to me like a man would." He seemed to be waiting for someone who was similar to me to show him what it was like to be in a relationship with a real lady.

I arched up to greet him, enjoying the perfect touch of morning sunlight on my skin. Now that the heated projectile was pushing me to the edge, the warmth was a welcome bonus. He stood up slightly and proceeded to massage the shaft against the small bud that had developed a voice. He had a certain independence about him and was my wild, wild child.

"That's it, just keep doing what you're doing; don't stop. That manhood is amazing. You can't imagine how much

I've missed interacting with others. Get your tongue down here to suck my nipples and fuck me. He obeyed my instructions, and I appreciated how easy he could be trained. "Now slow down..speed up." It was intriguing to accompany him the entire distance and continue to sense the pulsating long vein behind his cock, urging him to let go of the contents of his balls.

"I am... CUMMMMMING." Seeing his face morph into a mask of passion and longing was adorable. To feel his loins yield to what he'd spent so much time attempting to hide from me. A few spurts of hot seed that appeared to appear out of nowhere penetrated my body. He finally laid down on top of me after a few moments of pure bliss, his cock pulsating with an energy of its own.

His childlike joy didn't take long to rear its ugly head once more. He shifted me so that I was on my hands and knees, clutching the same stand in the palm of my hand, with my breasts forced into the stand.

"Lynn, I appreciate how responsive you are. You are so much more attractive than women my own age." As he pulled me in closer, I felt his hand on my hips and his balls bouncing obscenely against my lips. He then slipped back into the saddle. "I don't know how I'm going to be able to stop myself from blowing my load again, you are so damn hot." Because he had previously evacuated what he had and it would take some time for him to generate more, I knew exactly how he was going to do it.

It was everything I had imagined and more when I heard his hips smacking my rolled over ass. He yanked my hair and made me squeal with a certain belief that comes from knowing that he was the man with the stamina. He was deeper than he was when I was on my back. Most likely, he could keep up with any woman.

"Asshole me... God darn it, I'm fucked. He had yanked my hair and forced me to gaze at him the entire while he was prodding his hips up into me, so I could tell he was grinning. He was clearly demonstrating to me that age was just a number, and I could still feel that sensation of being desired and lusted after.

Still, there was no time for deep thinking. I shot into the shadows once more, then doubled back into the kitchen and hurriedly rounded the corners of the counters. It was fairly easy to avoid the shots because I created such widespread chaos that they were hardly able to figure out where the shots were coming from.

I went back into the kitchen and dealt two more blows to the guys in the living room, bringing them to the ground. Fortunately, I had the upper hand and shot both of their companions as the man inside the hallway came charging after them. Fred came howling and roaring from down behind the men. With his teeth clenched, he tramped all over the men.

There were still two gunmen, and they shot me again. Once again, I ducked behind the counter, which had been reinforced to withstand any situation similar to this one, and maintained a low profile while maintaining a stable back. I would just fire and kill these, too, in a matter of seconds.

I heard a snap, so I quickly looked into the room to see what was going on. Fred was snapping the men's necks while he was on his haunches and both hind legs. He split them in two by slamming his tail into their chests. I observed as their bodies gave way under the force of Fred's tail, his strength and rage acting like a blitzkrieg. Invincible. I was not going to be the object of Fred's wrath!

More people came to knock on the door. With my gun aimed at anyone who dared to enter, I leaned forward. My aim was focused on hitting the first person to pass through. No forgiveness.

Not for these dickhead sons of pricks.

With his head down and tail swaggering, Fred growled at the door. His hips were stiff, as though he could leap at any time and strike anyone at any time.

I muttered, "I'll get them," as my legs trembled and beads of sweat ran down my cheeks. It originated from the corners of my lips, from my eyebrows. I stayed wobbly on the countertops, where my elbows trembled. "I'll obtain them."

There was a burst of gunfire as the door exploded. As bullets rained down on us, I made the conscious decision to duck in order to protect myself. Fred dashed into the kitchen, shielding himself from their gunshots by covering the sink. Then he took off, back-flopping onto the attackers who went after us, his tail severing their necks like he was using a scythe rather than a bone or tissue. I ducked around the corner, aimed at one of the men to the left, and squeezed the trigger again, sending another bullet straight into his face. Blood squirted out from his throat, came dribbling down his chest in a massive flow. I fired another blast and landed two more shots on a couple of guys outside. The humans fell backwards, stumbling over themselves, tripping and tripping.

Fred raised his tail, slamming it into another nearby person. He swept under their legs, knocking them over before they could run away. Then he chased the remnant human forces, running down the halls, his wolf howling inside me, my head, ringing like a bell, an incessant noise.

"Dammit," I said, aiming my gun once more. I fired a couple of last rounds to make sure that these humans could never get up again. That they were truly good and dead. Once I figured out that they were, I went over to the doorway, and stuck my head out, just to see what was happening.

"Fucker," someone said from behind, wrapping their arms around my neck. Suddenly, I choked and couldn't breathe any longer. My lungs were forced of air, my legs were cycling as if I were on a bicycle. The gun fell from my hand, and I glanced up and to my sides. No longer was Fred around to protect me. I had to figure this out on my own...

Or so I thought, because Fred had been in the shadows watching, and now he came leaping, jumping for me, knocking the man who choked me away. I fell to the ground, on a body, blood on my chest and my mouth. I spat, sweating through my shirt, my skin slicked in gore. Running back inside, I heard gunshots, the sound of bullets striking the countertops, hitting the hallways, hitting Fred. Then Fred yelled out, growling, snarling, and he sunk his teeth into the man, ripping out his heart, tearing it away and stomping him against a wall as if he were nothing but a toy to play with.

"Yes," I said, under my breath. "The stupid bastards..."

Fred raked his teeth across the man's body, sinking in deeper and deeper until I saw his mouth completely bloodied, as if he now had a sandwich of blood, cresting from his chin to his chest. He shook his head out, ripping the man in half. Served him good and right.

I walked over to Fred, crouching low, making sure that he was okay. But Fred stared at me, his head bruised and battered.

"What actions should I take?" I said, scanning the area intently to see if someone was waiting to attack us once more. With these attacks against werewolves, you can never be too sure. Humans were not above using pipe bombs and unexpected mass killings, and they knew how to act dirty.

I detested my own kind for their brutality. However, we managed to evolve with werewolves in this way. by engaging in violent combat.

Fred changed, turning to face me while gasping and shaking his shoulders and legs. "We are able to... We can head to my workspace. That's the safest area to be.

I was encouraged to walk by his touch on my behind. Instead, I fled out of fear for what might occur. The following few seconds were pure terror.

However, I needed to concentrate and realign my thinking. The last thing I wanted to do at a moment like this was panic. I continued to move my legs and feet forward, pushing into the darkness one step at a time and turning out any lights that the men had turned on.

Inside Fred's space, with his four steel-and-concrete reinforced office walls, we gave way. It makes sense why he desired for us to be within. The same kind of weapons were in my bedroom too, but I assumed Fred was concealing other things.

He said, "In here," as he shut the door behind me. I swiftly moved to sit in front of his desk so that my legs could rest. I collapsed onto the chair's sides, clutching my tummy with my fingers while I took slow, deliberate breaths in and out. "That was absurd."

"Definitely," I said. "What took place? How were they able to outwit us? The CIA is where?

Fred stated, "They're still downstairs." However, I was unable to communicate with them. I'm no longer in direct communication. Thus, we will attempt to contact them immediately.

He logged onto his computer and started typing rapidly, his expression full of aggressive intention. I gazed at him as creases appeared on his forehead, his thoughts racing a thousand miles per hour, considering every possible way to reconnect with our crew in Angola.

Even though I'm not religious, I said a little prayer to anyone who could hear me just then.

This was horrible news for Henley and Rebecca; if the humans had attacked us unexpectedly, that was bad news indeed. Did they all make it out okay? If they were going to face their enemies, where were they going?

Had they lost their way? Had they been forced to kneel, implore each other? Should we go try to save them?

We are lying next to each other, both of us completely naked. We are transparent and nude. We seem to be exactly where we ought to have been a long time ago. I stroke his face and compliment him on his beauty. He brushes my hair out of my eyes, bends in, and gives me a kiss on the lips that is as gentle as a butterfly's fluttering wings. I move to be inside his shielding arms and give him a kiss in return. As his tongue glides between my lips and caresses my own, he seizes control of this kiss as well. Our bodies are united by a heat that simultaneously burns and calms us, entwining our legs. He's getting harder against me, and I can feel myself getting harder too, straining against his stomach. He drags his hands down my chest and stomach, sucking at my neck. I become even more rigid in his hands as he rubs me.

I suck at his earlobe, leaning in close. In the hopes that nothing will change for him, I mumble what I have to say. "This is a new experience for me."

When he draws back from his long, passionate kiss, he says, "Neither have I, not with the person I'm supposed to be with, not with the person I am forever imprinted on." He looks into my eyes first.

I'm melting into his touch, and I know that this will end far too quickly if I don't focus. "Please enter my body." I beseech him to consummate the connection as I gaze up at him through my eyelashes.

I could almost finish just feeling him against me as he tenderly pulls me into his lap. He is really firm beneath me. "Thomas, I love you and I will take care of you." He leans over and runs his tongue up and down my shaft as he gently places me down in front of him. I stroke his hair with my hands and hunch down, holding his broad shoulders. Before he lets me emerge from his mouth, he takes me between his lips and gives me a long, hard suck. I groan as he buries my pulsing sex in his throat once more, then rubs his tongue over its head. Before I know it, I'm trembling against him as he kisses me all over till he ends up back in my mouth. "Baby, roll over." I find myself on all fours as he pushes me in the direction he wants and runs his powerful hands all over my back. As I get more at ease, he gently starts to pump out a rhythm that gets faster. He drives himself in and out of me and grips my shoulders because it feels so nice inside of me. He accelerates as his breathing gets more rapid. He trembles against me and settles down, breathing in and out slowly until he is motionless inside of me. He puts his arms around me and rests his head on my back. I cup one hand behind my back to his face. We stay like this for a few minutes before we ultimately part ways. He spreads his wings and beckons me into his arms. I laid in his arms, caressing his stomach and chest with my hand.

"I apologise it took so long for that to happen," he says at the end. It was somewhat enchanted. I snicker at how bashful he suddenly appears to be in light of everything.

"It had a magical quality." I stroke my fingertip over the massive scar that occupies half of his face while staring into his eyes. "How did this come to pass? And this, too? I start at his shoulder and move my fingers along the arm that has a terrible burn mark on it.

After a long period of silence, I begin to worry that perhaps I said something incorrectly. It's possible that he doesn't want to discuss this and that my asking was inappropriate. At last, he starts talking. "It took place in the Navy." I lost everything in an attack on the ship I was on, including my career. He takes hold of my hand and puts it to his lips, kissing my fingers many times in a gentle manner. "Some of those sailors lost everything; some of them lost more than I did."

I give him a firm hug in the hopes that my hug will provide him some consolation. I lay there with him for as long as I feel comfortable before telling him it's time for us to move because there are joggers passing by this stretch of the beach in the morning.

Fortunately, I always have enough clothes in my backpack to last us both until we can return home. To get to the spot where he parked his car on the side of the road, we have to walk about one mile. After dropping me off at my flat, he promises to phone me when he gets back from his much-needed sleep. He drives me there. The following night, when we are both off from work, I make him a promise that I will prepare a dinner similar to the ones my mother used to make for him.

I go upstairs and am met with an approving Stonewall who gives me a "where the hell have you been" kind of look. I give him a head pat and fill his bowl with food and water. He appears to be rather understanding. I get rid of the sand that has stuck to my body with a brief shower, and a comfy cushion puts me to sleep. I'm in shock at how incredible last night was.

All of a sudden, though, everything fit together. Like a bomb, his consciousness burst forth, taking in everything at once. All the wolves in the group.Jace and Tabitha. Francine's maddening leaping motion. Every dread and every hope.Zena was protected by Dirk's shield.

He noticed that everything was connected as time slowed. He was amazed at Helmut. He saw what appeared to be a dozen firefly trails encircling him against the dusk sky. He became startled upon realizing those were the traces of his movements. He could sense Helmut's goal as he inhaled the slow motion.

In an attempt to rip Daniel's ear off his head, Helmut started to rip back. He had to let it go, he realized. He didn't feel depressed when he let Helmut turn around and noticed the firefly trail leading to his location. Then came the trail of his intended destination. With the ear in his lips, Helmut threw back his head, revealing his throat.

Daniel then leaped. Daniel twisted up beside Helmut's leaping spiral, positioning his body to meet his and his mouth wide to touch Helmut's bare throat.

He located Helmut's jugular easily, like a slow-motion dance, and clamped his fangs around it. Taking his place in the future and aligning himself with it felt as simple as following a thread.

Then he took a bite. He firmly broke through Helmut's artery as time returned to its life-speed, savouring the hot, abundant spray of blood that covered his muzzle. With a quick shake of his head, he severed the vessel beyond repair.

Shocked, Helmut looked around as he fell into a heap. His features froze as the realization that he was dying and that he had been battered struck him with horror. As the light dimmed, Daniel let go of his throat and raised his gaze to meet his, giving him a determined look.

Daniel sat heavily in the dirt, gasping, trails of blood running from his open mouth and the gaping cut where his ear had been, until he was positive that Helmut was dead. With caution, the group moved closer to him. He sensed their curiosity, fear, and shock.

He moved and stood up, shaking his head. A number of other wolves also changed, while some, unable to control their panic, repeatedly changed from human to wolf and again.

"Everyone, everyone!" he exclaimed, extending his hands. "Please try to remain composed. I'm not sure why, but Helmut

"I comprehend!" Torrin yelled. "You're the new Alpha here!"

"What?" Daniel barked. "No, Grant.

Francine cried out, "Grant's dead!" as her tawny wolf changed. "You and Helmut volunteered,"

"No!" Zena screamed. "Grant lives on!"

Francine sprung to attention, growling, and moved right away. With a gasp, Zena also changed, defensively springing up on her hind legs. Francine pawed the ground, hunched her shoulders, and let out a wild howl. She suddenly ducked, poised to attack. She lunged towards Zena's direction. Immediately, Dirk transformed and flung himself at her, sending her hurtling through the air as his massive form knocked her down. Her body broke against the old fence post's rusted spike, legs flailing towards the heavens. Her frame went slack and landed on the gravel and weeds without even a murmur.

Dirk turned human again and sprinted in Francine's direction. Helplessly, he raised his arms and clenched his fists. With gratitude,

Zenachanged and raced to his side, collapsing into his arms.

"She's not alive!" As Daniel rushed forward, Dirk muttered, startled. Francine gazed up at the sky with her golden eyes fixedly fixed. Daniel instinctively looked for her in the soul-space and discovered that, indeed, she had vanished.

"That's unbelievable!" said Dirk. "What did I do?"

Daniel regrettably shook his head. Dirk, you had to defend your cub. as well as your partner.

In unison, the pack said, "We know this is true."

Daniel let out a deep breath and spoke up to the group. "Francine's spirit is no longer with us. In brighter days, we shall cherish her memory and keep her affection close to our hearts.

"We are aware of this fact."

With his arms wrapped around Zena, Dirk breathed deeply into her shoulder. His grief spread like a radio emergency, bringing the pack together in regret and compassion. They will miss Francine, of course, but they knew deep down that he had done what needed to be done.

With uncertainty, the group moved through their positions, unsure of what to do next. Daniel stumbled across the parking lot, pulling his jeans and boots back on. He hesitantly put his hand to his head and felt the jagged flesh of his ripped ear with compassion. Tabitha's fingers was gripping her throat as she lay where she had fallen. Jace held her close and protectively.

"Tabitha!" Daniel cried out. "Oh my god... Is she aware of this?" he asked Jace.

Jace refused to look away from her. "She's awake," he whispered. Seldom. Man, what the fuck?

When Daniel attempted to connect with her through the soul-space, Jace had her firmly and impenetrably wrapped around him.

Hello, what's going on? he murmured.

However, he was aware of this beforehand. With a resolute glance, Tabitha met Jace's eyes as if he were a lighthouse beam piercing the mist. Daniel recognised that expression. Grant had stared at him in the same manner the night he realised he was his buddy.

"You better take good care of her," he moaned, his happiness starting to blossom.

Is that what my Alpha is telling me to do? Jace gave a snarky reply.

"Yes, whatever," Daniel replied as he sat firmly in the mud and felt fatigue suddenly overtake him like a dark cloud. "I'm not an Alpha."

Jace pointed with his chin towards the pack and replied, "Oh, I think you are." They gathered in a half circle about him, fervently professing their love to him.

Dirk nodded and said, "I think so too."

Zena answered, "Yes, you are."

Twelve heads nodding, sorrowful yet hopeful at the same time, confirming what he suspected. Then there was a different voice.

He said, "I'll call you Alpha."

Daniel sprang up and flung himself into his partner's arms. Grant staggered back, nearly stopping his fall.

"Oh, I'm sorry!" Daniel stammered pitifully. "Oh my god, it's you!"

Grant merely nodded before encircling Daniel in his arms. He let out a deep sigh, and Daniel could feel the fatigue in his body.

He whispered, "They need you to say something."

Daniel looked up at the group of people. Everybody looked at him attentively and with curiosity. Nobody spoke at all. Gripping Zena firmly, Dirk's look was one of shock, grief, and resolve.

Daniel lifted his voice and continued, "Everyone, I want you to know that Crane was like a father to me." Francine is like a mother to me. I was upset that I had no relatives when I first arrived, but I made an effort to accept Crane's family. Although Crane once told me that the Alpha must love every member of his pack as though they were his own blood, I never truly grasped what he was training me for. That wasn't how I felt till today. I feel kinship with all of you today. It gives me courage and a sense of obligation. I get it now. All of you are my blood.

He looked from face to face, accepting without reservation each person's promise of love and commitment. Their happiness filled him with purpose and swept over him like a refreshing wave.

"But as we move forward, I would like to make a change," he acknowledged. "Because Grant is my Alpha no matter what." I was never going to break that bond. He could see that this was correct as he looked into Grant's green eyes.

"So I would like to tell him about this!"

A look of confusion flashed across the group. Torrin shrugged, but Zena gave a firm nod.

"A pair of alphas!" Pumping his fist high in the air, Torrin yelled.

The pack's response was, "Two Alphas!"

Raise your fists, everyone, and express your love and solidarity in both your human and wolf forms. "We know this is true!" was the joyful yell they all let out at once.

Why was I unable to say it?

Caster was in the garage, starting to worry about whether Simon would indeed show up for practice. If only he could have said those words last night.

Caster had wanted Simon from the first instant he had seen him. Though

Caster had started to feel a different kind of yearning for Simon yesterday, he had still wanted to grab his tight little omega ass and make it his.

Why was it that I was unable to express to him my true feelings for him?

Caster closed his eyes and used his thumb and fingertip to massage his temples. He had dated a number of men and women in the past, and each had served only as a vehicle for gratifying a sexual craving. Alongside Caster... It was unfamiliar to him to feel this way about anyone.

"Are you prepared?"

Caster jerked out of his reverie at the sound of Simon's voice. The doors had not even opened for him. He said, "Simon." Simon was taking off his clothing as soon as he unlocked the cupboard. "I simply desired to-"

Simon cut in, "C'mon." He closed his eyes, and his body exploded, changing into a wolf. He had already mastered the change in a single day. "Go out and race you."

Caster hastily undressed as Simon bounded off like a bolt of white lightning. His feet thudded on the concrete floor, giving him a running start, and he sank on his all fours like a wolf. Even though Simon managed to acclimatize to the shift, Caster swiftly closed the distance since he was still out of sync with his body. With tongues flapping furiously, they bolted out of the waterfall exit as the garage door slid open.

Caster thought, I don't know how to tell him. However, perhaps...I could demonstrate to him.

He said, "Follow me," and started to run.

Caster launched himself off the trail and into a gully. They hopped from rock to rock to bridge a stream, then lunged through dense undergrowth and low-lying branches to reach the other side.

"Where are we heading?" Simon gave a call.

"Somewhere special," Caster said, scuttling into the undergrowth.

Simon ran for what seemed like miles in pursuit of Caster. Now, they had ventured far farther into the park than they had done the day before, deep into the woods. The excitement he had felt when he had first become a wolf was still there, but it was now overshadowed by contradictory emotions that seemed to follow him about. How could his feelings about another man be this? It was one thing to want to fuck, but Simon had never felt anything like this towards a woman.

A small voice within his skull said, "It's love."

No, he thought, how could that be? Caster is a male individual. I mean, how could I fall in love with a man?

The small voice added, "Think about Kevin and what you did with him."

He believed that was different.

Caster yelled, "Almost there," and skidded to a stop. Distracted, Simon almost ran him over. They had reached an overgrown trail that was hardly discernible through the thick undergrowth. "Get moving."

After some time of meandering through the jungle, they came to a clearing that Simon could see in the distance. His nose detected the smell of something artificial, and he soon saw it: a verdant meadow clearing in the middle of a forest, with a charming-looking house tucked away. It had the feel of something from a book.

Simon said, "What is this place?" with wonder.

Caster remarked, "Somewhere that I've never shown anyone else before." Around them, meadow grass and wildflowers gently waved in the breeze as birds chirped sweetly. When he got to the door, he transformed back into a human, and Simon did the same. Caster unlatched the exquisite and substantial oak front door, allowing them to enter the property. Simon couldn't resist taking a sly peek at Caster's toned and muscular posterior.

His breath left him on the inside. It was quite elegant and understated. There was a genuine feeling of tranquility in this location. There was a little bed, a cast iron stove in the corner and an unfinished wooden table and chair. A window with crown glass panes let in a flood of white light, which illuminated the floor and table in a rectangle glow. He had the impression of entering a Vermeer painting.

Caster remarked, "This is where I come when I want to be alone," taking a robe from the dresser and giving it to Simon before donning his own. "It serves as my haven when the outside world gets too much to bear."

Simon sat down in the wooden chair and remarked, "It's hard to imagine a man like you having a hard time handling anything." "Have you created this?"

Caster grinned. "How were you aware of this?"

"I'm not sure. I was reminded of you by something about it. Perhaps the rawness of it.

Simon met Caster's eyes directly. He didn't feel like he had to turn away for the first time. There was only a powerful, overwhelming sensation of desire; intimidation had vanished. Simon felt his heart race. Regardless of his gender, this sensation is genuine.

"You're unique, which is why I wanted to show you this place," Caster remarked, glancing off into space.

When Simon extended his hand to touch Caster's hand that was resting on the table, it trembled a little. A surge of electricity shot through Simon as his fingertips touched Caster's hand on the back. For Simon, it was the one thing in the world he had ever wanted—the first time their bodies had ever touched.

Caster winced, jerking his head and expressing a momentary look of astonishment before relaxing. He lifted his hand and took Simon's. As Simon glanced up at the man he had fallen in love with, he felt as though his heart would burst out of his chest. Caster pulled Simon into his arms and to his feet with a swift motion of his hand. Caster kissed Simon before he could say anything by bringing him close to him and sliding his hand around the back of his head.

As Caster's lips touched Simon's, the walls in his heart and mind collapsed to dust, and he put his arms around the towering alpha's neck, drawing himself even more into him. With a swift movement, Caster hauled Simon up onto the table, knocking the chair across the floor. Caster snarled, "I want you,

Simon," and Simon gave vent to a longing whimper. All he needed to hear was that.

He stared into Caster's eyes intently until a hunger pandemic struck. Eagerly untying the knot, he caught Caster by the robe's belt and pulled his waist in closer. God, I really can't contain it anymore. Right now, I need it. As Caster straightened, he noticed the robe gathering at the top. He inhaled deeply, letting Caster's cozy fragrance seep through the material. "You have a delicious smell," he said.

Caster placed his hands on his hips and invited Simon to have complete control over him, grinning amorously as he stared down at Simon. Simon paused briefly, filled with eager expectation, before lowering the robe's belt. His eyes widened as Caster's cock broke free, revealing a completely different beast than the one he had witnessed during their transformation. The two sides fell open. It is fully erect and firm with arousal. Simon was greeted with the full enticing scent of his manhood as the tip glistened with a bead of pre-come.

Simon licked his lips and became very fixated on Caster's massive cock, which was directly in front of his face. At that moment, he realized that there was nothing else that could satisfy him. Without further delay, he parted his lips widely.

***